TeeJay Publishers

TJ Publishers
Advantage Business Centre
132-134 Great Ancoats Street
Manchester
M4 6DE

Tel: 0141 880 6839
Fax: 0870 124 9189
e-mail: teejaypublishers@btinternet.com
web page: www.teejaypublishers.co.uk

© TeeJay Publishers 2014
 First Edition published by TeeJay Publishers - January 2014

All rights in this book are reserved. No part of this book may be copied
or reproduced in any format, including electronic, without the express
permission of the authors in accordance with the Copyright, Design
and Patents Act of 1988.

Any person or organisation who makes unauthorised copies of any part
of this book may be liable to prosecution and possible civil claims for
damages.

Printed by :-

Elanders Ltd
Merlin Way
New York Business Park
North Tyneside NE27 0QG
Registered in England number 3788582
 http://www.elanders.com/uk

Year 1
Textbook
Book 1A

Produced by members of the TeeJay Writing Group

T Strang, J Geddes and J Cairns.

TeeJay would like to thank *Caoimhe Ni Chomhrai* and *Rachel Phazey* for their invaluable advice, recommendations and help with this book.

Front and Back Cover and web-site designed by *Fraser McKie*.
(http://www.frasermckie.com)

Characters in the book developed and drawn by
Susan Fitzpatrick and *Karen Anna Sandholm*.

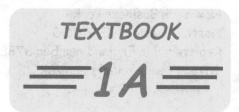

TEXTBOOK
1A

National Curriculum TextBook 1A

- This book, along with Textbook 1B covers every outcome of the Year 1 course, as laid out in the National Curriculum England framework document, (September 2013).

- There are no A and B exercises. The book covers the first half of the Year 1 course without the teacher having to pick and choose which questions to leave out and which exercises are important. They all are !

- The book follows on directly from TeeJay's 12 Reception Booklets A1-A12.

- Year 1 Book 1A contains a 5 page "Chapter Zero" which primarily revises every topic from our Reception course and can be used as a diagnostic tool. This could be followed by TeeJay's diagnostic assessments * of the work covered in our Year 1 books.

- Non-calculator skills are emphasised and encouraged throughout the book.

- Each chapter will have a "Revisit - Review - Revise" exercise as a summary.

- Homework*, mirroring exercise by exercise, the topics in this book, is available as a photocopiable pack.

- TeeJay's Assessment Pack* for Year 1 work, is also available as a photocopiable pack, and can be used topic by topic or combined to form a series of Year 1 Cumulative Tests. It also contains a series of longer assessments covering the Outcomes as laid out in the National Curriculum England framework document.

We make no apologies for the multiplicity of colours used throughout the book, both for text and in diagrams - we feel it helps brighten up the pages !!

T Strang, J Geddes, J Cairns

(January 2014)

* Available for purchase separately.

Contents

The Family

Mr Duff   Mrs Todd   Mr Todd   Miss Smart

Denzel   Willis   Ravi   Nick   Ben   Spot   Lucy   Jane   Jemma   Sarah   Ella

Tiddles

Revision

1. Which one is **smaller** (a or b) ?

2. Which one is **bigger** ?

3. Which one is **heavier** ?

4. Which one is **lighter** ?

5. Who is **taller** - Sarah or Ben ?

6. Which is **shorter** - pen or pencil ?

7. Which holds **more** - kettle or basin ?

8. How many ?

a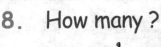

b

9. a How many **more** to make 7 ?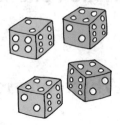

b  How many **more** to make 10 ?

10. What are the **missing** numbers ?

a 3   4   5   6   7   (?)   9.

b 10   9   8   (?)   6   5   4.

11. Write these numbers in order.

Start with the **smallest**.

12. a Write the number **1 more** than **4**.

  b Write the number **1 less** than **8**.

13. How many sweets do Ben and Nick have **altogether** ?

Ben

Nick

14. Jane has **7** apples.

  She gives **2** apples to Tom.

  How many apples has she left ?

15. Draw the **next** shape in these patterns :-

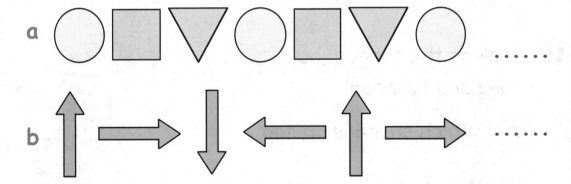

a ⬤ ◻ ▽ ⬤ ◻ ▽ ⬤ ......

b ⬆ ➡ ⬇ ⬅ ⬆ ➡ ......

16. Write the name of each **shape**.

  (Choose from :- circle, square, triangle, rectangle).

  a ◻   b ▭   c ⬤   d ▷

17. Write the name of each **object**.

(Choose from cone, pyramid, cylinder, cube).

a 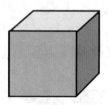   b    c 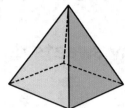   d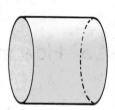

18. a   Which fruit is **just in front** of the melon ?

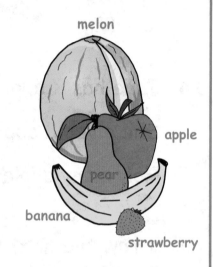

b   Which fruit is **just behind** the strawberry ?

c   Which fruit is **at the back** ?

19. Look at the cube, cuboid, cone and cylinder.

a   Which shape is **on top** ?

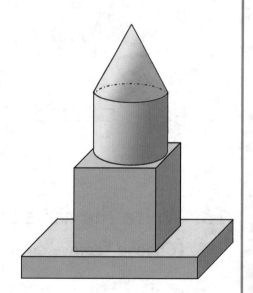

b   Which shape is **just above** the cube ?

c   Which shape is **just below** the cube ?

20. Look at the
    farm animals.

    a   Which animal is **on the very left** ?

    b   Which animal is **just to the right** of the pig ?

    c   Which animal is **just to the left** of the cow ?

    d   Which animal is **in the middle** ?

21. a   How many **children** ?

    b   How many **girls** ?

    c   How many **boys
        wearing glasses** ?

22. Mugs in the dinner hall.

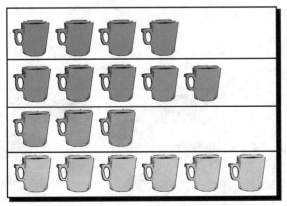

    a How many **green** mugs ?

    b How many **blue** mugs ?

    c How many mugs
       altogether ?

    d How many **more yellow**
       mugs than **red** mugs ?

Chapter 1

Numbers from 0 to 10

Be able to count to 10, forwards and backwards.

Revision :-

You should be able to count from 1 to 10 by now.

Example 1 :-

How many lollies ?

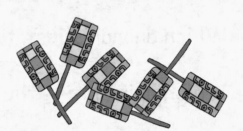

Point and count them like this :-   1 - 2 - 3 - 4 - 5 - 6 .

Example 2 :-

What are the missing numbers here ?

1 - 2 - 3 - ☐ - 5 - 6 - 7 - ☐ - 9 - ☐

By counting, the missing numbers are 4 8 and 10 .

Exercise 1

1. How many ?

a

b
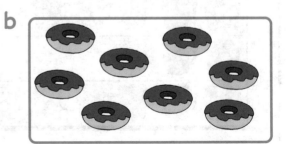

1. c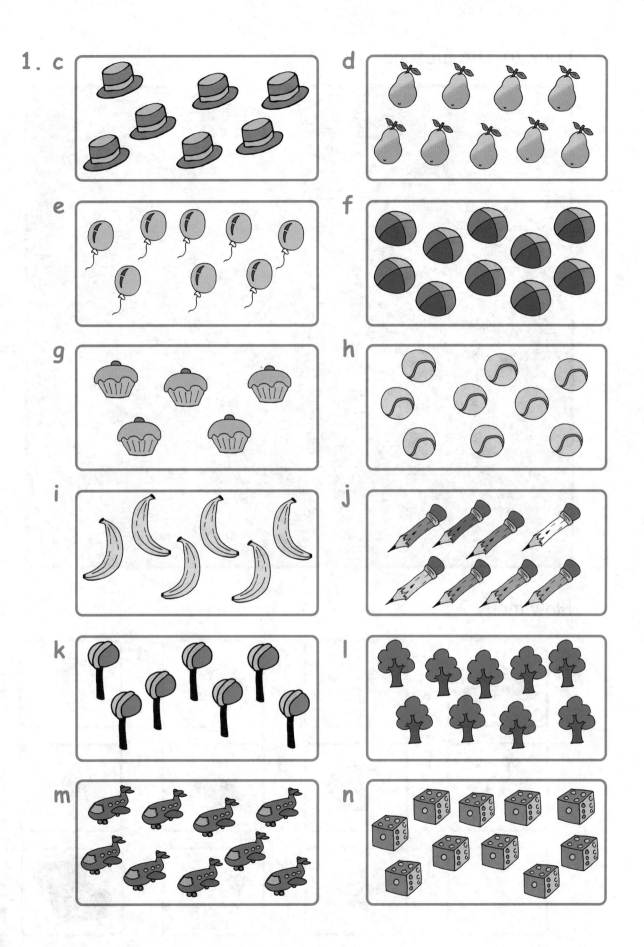

2. Look at the picture.

How many ?

3. What are the missing numbers ?

a 1 - 2 - 3 - ☐ - 5 - ☐ - 7 - ☐ - ☐ - 10

b 1 - ☐ - 3 - ☐ - ☐ - 6 - 7 - 8 - 9 - ☐

c 1 - ☐ - ☐ - 4 - 5 - 6 - ☐ - 8 - ☐ - 10

d ☐ - 2 - ☐ - 4 - ☐ - 6 - ☐ - 8 - ☐ - 10

e 10 - 9 - ☐ - 7 - ☐ - 5 - ☐ - 3 - ☐ - 1

f 10 - ☐ - 8 - ☐ - ☐ - ☐ - 4 - 3 - ☐ - 1

g 1 ☐ 3   h 3 ☐ 5

i 9 ☐ 7   j 10 ☐ 8

k ☐ 2 ☐ 4   l 10 ☐ ☐ 7.

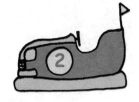  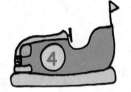 

4. What is the number which lies **between** :-

a   3 and 5   b   0 and 2   c   7 and 9

d   8 and 10   e   4 and 2   f   6 and 4 ?

5. Write down the **two numbers** which lie **between** :-

a   4 and 7   b   1 and 4   c   6 and 3

d   9 and 6   e   7 and 10   f   8 and 5.

6. Write down each list, starting with the **lowest** number :-

a   7   2   6   4   b   8   1   9   10   5

c   8   9   3   7   4   d   9   6   10   4   7   8.

7. Write down each list, (**highest** number first) :-

a   3   5   2   6   b   8   4   2   9   7

c   7   10   8   9   d   5   2   7   8   4   9.

8. What are the missing numbers here ?

a   0 - ☐ - ☐ - 6 - ☐ - 10

b   ☐ - ☐ - 5 - 3 - ☐ .

Numbers from 0 to 10 as Numerals and in Words

A number can be written in number form or as a word.

Here are the numbers from zero to ten in words :-

0 – zero		**1** – one		**2** – two	
3 – three		**4** – four		**5** – five	
6 – six		**7** – seven		**8** – eight	
9 – nine		**10** – ten			

Study them. Learn how to spell them.

Exercise 2

1. Write each of these in word form :-

    a 6   b 8   c 4   d 7
    e 3   f 9   g 2   h 10.

2. Write these in number form :-

    a seven   b one   c nine   d six
    e ten   f five   g three   h eight.

3. When a rocket is launched, the countdown begins
    ten - nine - eig..... - ......

    Write the countdown from ten to zero in words.

1.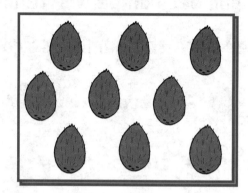

   a   How many fish ? (*Answer as a word*).

   b   How many coconuts ? (*Answer as a number*).

2. Write down the missing numbers :-

   a   1 - ☐ - ☐ - ☐ - 5 - ☐ - 7 - ☐ - ☐ - 10

   b   ☐ - ☐ - 8 - ☐ - ☐ - 5 - 4 - 3 - ☐ - ☐

   c   ☐ - 6 - 7 - ☐ - ☐ - 10.

3. What number lies between :-

   a   2 and 0   b   6 and 8   c   10 and 8 ?

4. Write down each list, (*highest number first*) :-

   a   4   8   10   6   b   3   1   7   9   5.

Be able to add up to 10 pictorially.

Number Bonds to 10 (Pictorially)

Example :-

Ben

Lucy

Ben has **5** Smarties.

Lucy has **3** Smarties.

Put together, Ben and Lucy have

| 5 | + | 3 | = | 8 | Smarties altogether. |

Exercise 1

1. Put together :-

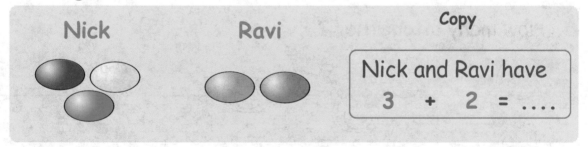

Nick   Ravi

Copy

Nick and Ravi have

3 + 2 = ...

2. How many altogether ?

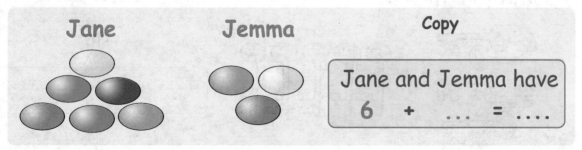

Jane   Jemma

Copy

Jane and Jemma have

6 + ... = ...

3. How many altogether ?

Ben   Jane   Copy

Ben and Jane have
5   +   ...   = ...

4. How many in total (*altogether*) ?

Anne   Tom   Copy

Anne and Tom have
3   +   ...   = ...

5. Put together :-

Copy

4   +   3   = ...

6. How many altogether ?

Copy

2   +   ...   = ...

7. Add together :-

Copy

...   +   ...   = ...

Number Bonds to 10

Be able to add up to 10.

Counters will help in this exercise.

Examples :-

| $5 + 1 = 6$ | $7 + 2 = 9$ |
| $8 + 0 = 8$ | $4 + 6 = 10$ |

Exercise 2   *Counters will help in this exercise.*    Worksheet 2·2

1. Put together 4 and 2.   Copy $4 + 2 = ...$

2. Put together :-

   a   2 and 6   b   8 and 1   c   4 and 3.

3. Add :-

   a $7 + 1 = ...$ b $9 + 0 ...$ c $1 + 5 = ...$

4. Find :-

   a $2 + 3$ b $6 + 2$ c $1 + 8$

   d $3 + 4$ e $4 + 5$ f $8 + 2.$

5. Add :-

   a $1 + 2 + 3$ b $1 + 3 + 2$ c $3 + 3 + 1$

   d $2 + 5 + 1$ e $3 + 3 + 2$ f $5 + 3 + 2.$

6. a   Jane has 7 coins. Lucy has 2 coins.

How many coins **altogether** ?

b   The boys have 4 coins. The girls have 4 coins.

How many coins do the children have **in total** ?

7. a      James has 3 teddy bears.
Sam has 4 teddy bears.

How many teddy bears **in total** ?

b   John has 5 pieces of pie. Alan also has 4.

How many pieces **altogether** ?

8. Mr Duff has 6 TJ books.
Miss Young has 4 TJ books.

How many when **put together** ?

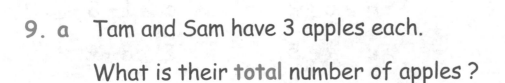

9. a   Tam and Sam have 3 apples each.

What is their **total** number of apples ?

b   Jane has **five** questions for homework.
Ben has **three** questions. Nick has **two**.

How many questions do they have **altogether** ?

Problem Solving (up to 10)

 Be able to solve problems with addition to 10.

Counters will help in this exercise.

Examples :- What are the missing numbers ?

$4 + \boxed{?} = 6$ $7 + \boxed{} = 7$

    $\boxed{2}$ is the missing number. $\boxed{0}$ is the missing number.

Exercise 3   *Counters will help in this exercise.*   **Worksheet 2·3**

1. What are the missing numbers ?

   a $2 + \boxed{} = 5$ b $1 + \boxed{} = 8$ c $7 + \boxed{} = 10$

   d $3 + \boxed{} = 9$ e $5 + \boxed{} = 7$ f $0 + \boxed{} = 7.$

2. What are the missing numbers ?

   a $\boxed{} + 4 = 5$ b $\boxed{} + 3 = 8$ c $\boxed{} + 4 = 10$

   d $\boxed{} + 7 = 9$ e $\boxed{} + 6 = 7$ f $4 + \boxed{} + 1 = 8.$

3. Lucy has **4** cakes. Ben has some cakes. Altogether they have **9** cakes.

   How many cakes does Ben have ?

4. 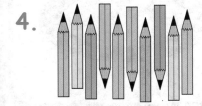 Bo has some pencils. He gets **2** more. Bo now has **10** pencils.

   How many did he start with ?

1. How many in total ?

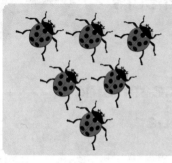 

... + 3 = ...

2. Find :-

a 5 + 1   b 3 + 2   c 4 + 3

d 5 + 3   e 3 + 7   f 4 + 2 + 3.

3. Ben has 6 worms. Ravi has 4 worms.

   How many worms altogether ?

4. Find the missing number :-

a 5 + ☐ = 6   b ☐ + 2 = 7   c ☐ + 4 = 9

d 1 + ☐ = 10   e ☐ + 8 = 8   f 3 + ☐ + 1 = 7.

5. Mr Todd washes some plates.
   Mrs Todd washes 4 plates.
   Altogether they wash ten plates.

   How many plates did Mr Todd wash ?

Chapter 3

Numbers from 10 to 20

Recognise and order numbers from 10 to 20.

Each full jar holds 10 sweets.

1 jar holding 7 sweets.   =   7 sweets.

1 full jar and 4 sweets.   =   14 sweets.

We have 2 full jars   =   20 sweets.

	ten	ones

The number 16 means 1 "lot" of ten and 6 ones.   **1 6**

Here are all the numbers from 10 to 20 :-

10	11	12	13	14	15	16	17	18	19	20

Exercise 1

1. How many sweets ?

a 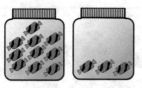   b   c

2. How many ?

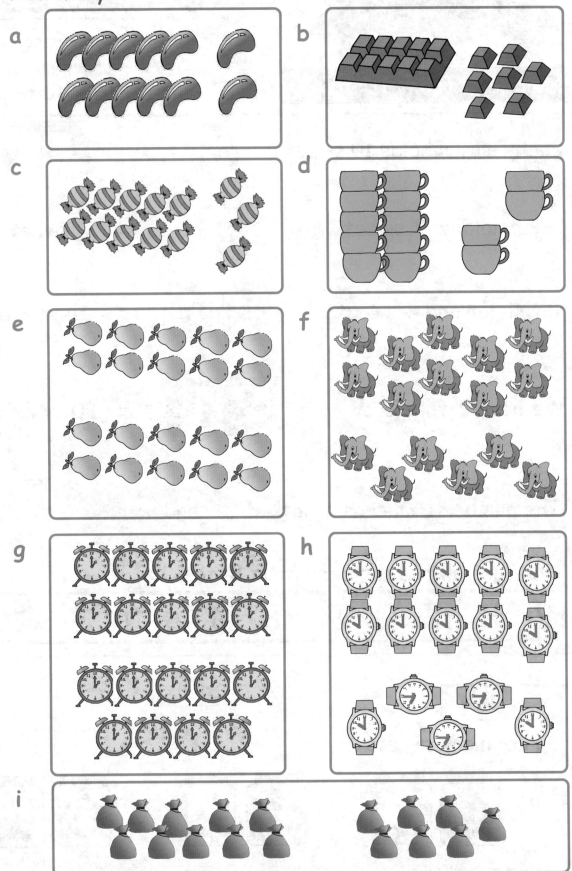

a

b

c

d

e

f

g

h

i

3. Look at the picture.

How many :-

a

b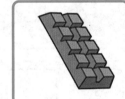

c

d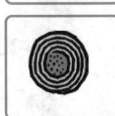

e

f

4. Draw or trace empty jars like this.

Fill them with round sweets to show :-

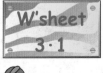

a	11	b	15	c	13	d	17
e	19	f	12	g	20	h	18.

5. What are the missing numbers ?

a   11 - 12 - ☐ - 14 - 15 - ☐ - 17 - ☐ - 19 - ☐

b   11 - ☐ - ☐ - ☐ - 15 - ☐ - 17 - 18 - ☐ - ☐

c   ☐ - 12 - ☐ - ☐ - 15 - ☐ - 17 - ☐ - 19 - ☐

d   20 - 19 - ☐ - 17 - ☐ - 15 - ☐ - ☐ - 12 - 11

e   20 - ☐ - 18 - ☐ - ☐ - ☐ - 14 - ☐ - 12 - 11

f   ☐ - 19 - ☐ - 17 - ☐ - ☐ - 14 - 13 - ☐ - ☐

g | 10 | 11 | ..... | 13 | ..... |

h | ..... | 15 | ..... | ..... | 18 |

i | 20 | ..... | ..... | 17 | ..... |

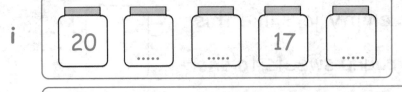

j | ..... | 19 | ..... | ..... | ..... | 15 | ..... |

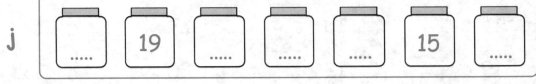

6. What is the number which lies **between** :-

a 10 and 12   b 15 and 17   c 14 and 16

d 20 and 18   e 19 and 17   f 13 and 11 ?

7. Write down the **two numbers** which lie **between** :-

a 11 and 14   b 16 and 19   c 17 and 14

d 20 and 17   e 12 and 9   f 15 and 18.

8. Write down each list, (*lowest number first*) :-

a   14   12   17   15   b   18   11   20   10   13

c   17   14   16   18   d   13   17   11   16   14.

9. Write down each list, (*highest number first*) :-

a   12   16   15   13   b   18   17   19   14   16

c   18   20   11   14   d   15   13   16   18   14.

10. **What** are the missing numbers here ?

a   6 - 8 - ☐ - ☐ - 14 - ☐ - 18

b   ☐ - ☐ - 15 - 13 - ☐ - 9 - ☐ - 5 .

10 to 20 as Words and as Numbers

Here are the numbers 10 to 20 written in word form :-

10 – ten   **11** – eleven   **12** – twelve

13 – thir<u>teen</u>   **14** – four<u>teen</u>   **15** – fif<u>teen</u>

16 – six<u>teen</u>   **17** – seven<u>teen</u>   **18** – eigh<u>teen</u>

19 – nine<u>teen</u>   **20** – twenty

Study them. **Learn** how to spell them.

Exercise 2

1. Write these in **word** form :-

a 16	b 18	c 14	d 17
e 13	f 19	g 12	h 20.

2. Write these in **number** form :-

a seventeen	b eleven	c nineteen	d sixteen
e twelve	f fifteen	g thirteen	h eighteen.

3. A race begins after counting **down** from 20.

   twenty - nineteen - eighteen - ......

   Write the countdown from **twenty**
   to **zero** in words.

1.

   a How many chicks ? (*Answer as a word*).

   b How many buttons ? (*Answer as a number*).

2. What are the missing numbers ?

   a 11 ☐ ☐ 14 15 ☐ 17 ☐ ☐ 20

   b ☐ 19 18 ☐ ☐ 15 14 ☐ 12 ☐

   c 11 ☐ ☐ 17 19 ☐.

3. What number lies between :-

   a 15 and 13   b 16 and 18   c 14 and 12 ?

4. Write down each list, (*lowest number first*) :-

   a 17 11 15 18   b 16 10 14 9 13.

Recognise and be able to name basic 2-D shapes.

Names of 2-D Shapes

You should know these shapes :-

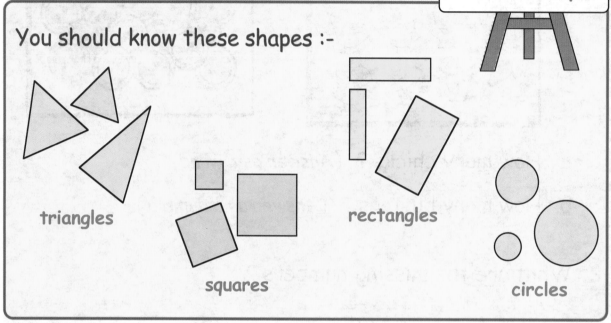

triangles

squares

rectangles

circles

Exercise 1

1. What is this shape called ? ⟶

2. ⟵ What is this shape called ?

3. What is this shape called ? ⟶

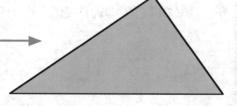

4. What is this shape called ? ——————→

5. Look at this picture :-

    a How many circles are there ?

    b How many squares ?

    c How many triangles ?

    d How many rectangles ?

    e How many pink circles are there ?

    f How many green triangles are there ?

    g How many red circles are there ?

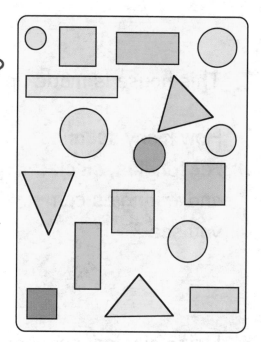

6. Look at the pictures below.

    What shapes can you see in them ?

    a    b 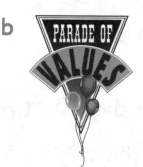   c    d

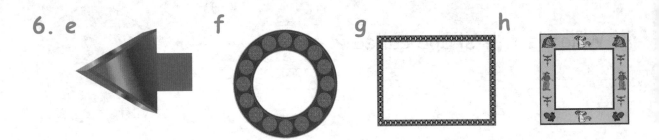

6. e　　　　　　f　　　　　g　　　　　h

7. This house is made up of shapes.

   How many squares,
   rectangles, circles
   and triangles can
   you see ?

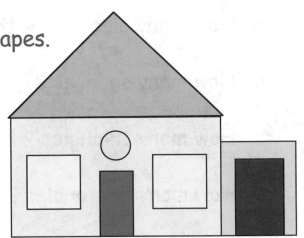

8. Using circles, squares, rectangles and triangles,
   draw a picture of :-

   a　　a robot　　　　　b　　a rocket　　　　c　　an aeroplane.

9. You can see a circle on a clock.

   List other places where you can see a :-

   a　　circle　　　　　b　　rectangle

   c　　square　　　　　d　　triangle.

10.a What is your favourite shape ?   Draw your shape.

   b Why did you pick this shape ?

Sides and Corners

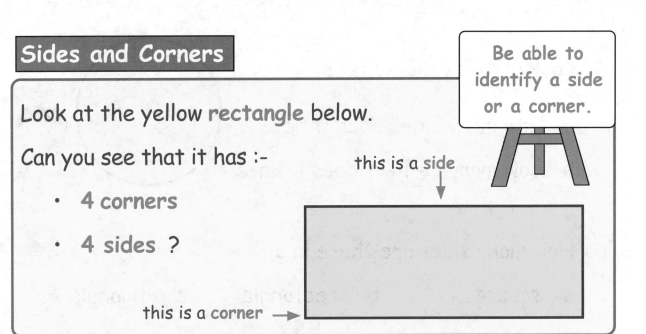

Be able to identify a side or a corner.

Look at the yellow **rectangle** below.

Can you see that it has :-

- **4 corners**

- **4 sides** ?

this is a side

this is a corner →

Exercise 2   *You will need a ruler.*

Worksheet 4·1

1. **Copy** this **square** and colour it in **green**.

    a   Write the word **side** next to each side.

    b   Write the word **corner** next to each corner.

2. **Copy** this **rectangle** and colour it in **blue**.

    a   Write the word **side** next to each side.

    b   Write the word **corner** next to each corner.

3. **Copy** this **triangle** and colour it in **pink**.

    a   Write the word **side** next to each side.

    b   Write the word **corner** next to each corner.

4. Look at this yellow circle :-

   a How many sides does it have ?

   b How many corners does it have ?

5. How many sides are there in a :-

   a square   b rectangle   c triangle ?

6. How many corners are there in a :-

   a square   b rectangle   c triangle ?

7. Copy or trace this shape and colour it.

   a How many sides does the shape have ?

   b How many corners does it have ?

   c Find out what the shape is called.

8. Copy or trace this shape and colour it in.

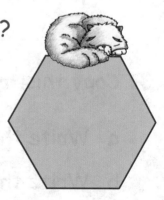

   a How many sides does the shape have ?

   b How many corners does it have ?

   c Find out what the shape is called.

9. a How many **sides** does this shape have ?

   b How many **corners** does it have ?

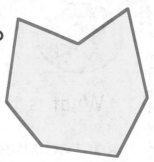

10. Look at these shapes :-

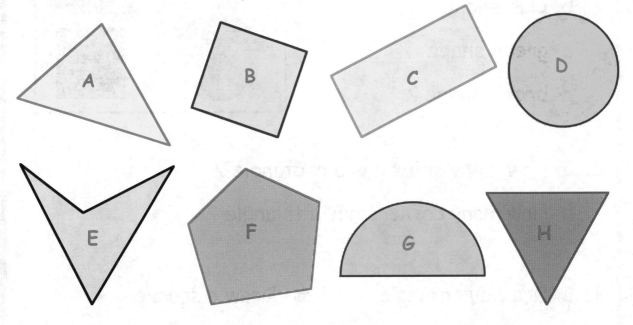

Which shapes have :-

a 4 sides   b 5 corners

c 1 curved side **only**   d 1 curved and
                                1 straight side ?

11. Draw and **colour** each of these shapes.

   A shape with :-

   a 3 sides   b 5 sides

   c 6 sides   d 4 corners

   e 8 corners   f 1 curved side.

1. What is the name of the :-

   a **red** shape

   b **blue** shape

   c **green** shape

   d **brown** shape ?

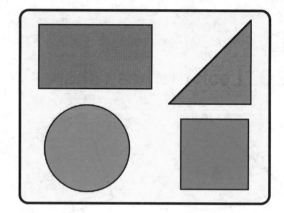

2. a How many **sides** has a rectangle ?

   b How many **corners** has a triangle ?

3. a Draw a rectangle.   b Draw a square.

   c Draw a triangle.   d Draw a circle.

4. a Use a ruler to draw a shape with **five** sides.

   b How many **corners** does your shape have ?

5. Write a list of things in your classroom
   where you see a rectangle.

6. Draw a picture using only squares, rectangles,
   triangles and circles.

One More/Less Than

Finding the number 1 more or 1 less than another number.

Lara is **7** years old.

Alison is **8** years old.

Alison is older than Lara,
because (8) is larger than (7).

Alison

Lara

Counting up from 5, 6, 7, ...
the number **8** is one up from 7.

Sandy is **11** years old.

Tommy is **10** years old.

Tommy is younger than Sandy,
because (10) is smaller than (11).

Tommy Sandy

Counting down from 20, 19, 18, ...
the number **10** is one down from 11.

Exercise 1

1. **Which is the larger ?** *Think of ages and which one is older.*

a 6 or 9	b 10 or 8	c 15 or 16
d 20 or 18	e 13 or 11	f 12 or 14.

2. Which is the **smaller** ?   *Think of ages and which one is younger.*

    a 7 and 5   b 11 and 12   c 15 and 18

    d 19 and 14   e 14 and 15   f 13 and 12.

3. Copy (or trace) each picture and draw
   in **one more** of each item.

a

b

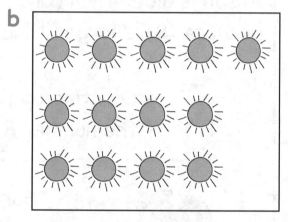

c

d

4. How many of these have you **now** :– (Check from your drawings)

    a beach balls   b shining suns

    c apples   d ducks ?

5. Write down the number one less than each of these :-

a

b

c
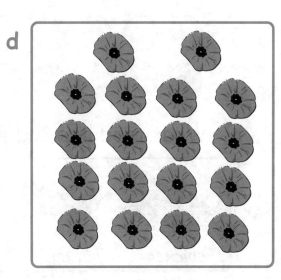

d

6. Write down the number that is **one more than** :-

a 7	b 11	c 18	d 15
e 12	f 19	g 13	h 10.

7. Write down the number that is **one less than** :-

a 17	b 3	c 18	d 9
e 12	f 16	g 11	h 13.

8. Fewer or More ?

   a   Which are there **more** of :- red dots or blue dots ?

   b   Which are there **fewer** of :- green or orange dots ?

   c   Which are there **more** of :- yellow or purple dots ?

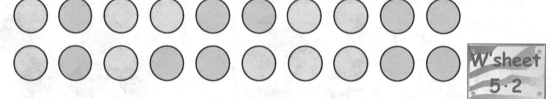

W'sheet 5·2

9. a   What food lies **2nd** from the **left** ? (*2 places in*).

5th place

chicken   hot dog   burger   sausage   roast

   b   Which boy is **4th** from the **left** ?

Willis   Ravi   Nick   Ben   Joe

   c   Which girl is **6th** from the **left** ?

Jane   Sarah   Anna   Jemma   Lara   Lucy

Some Word Problems

Exercise 2

1. Peppa jumped in **13** puddles going to school.

   She jumped in **1 more** than that coming home.

   How many puddles did she jump in coming home ?

2. Mr Davie lit **1** firework from his box.

   The box held **20** to begin with.

   How many is he left with ?

3. Sally has **12** mint toffees.

   Jason has **1** toffee **more** than that.

   How many toffees has Jason ?

4. The temperature in the morning was **18°**.

   By the afternoon, it was **1° less**.

   What was the temperature in the afternoon ?

5. Pam has **15** teddy bears in her room.

   Kate has **one fewer** than Pam.

   How many teddy bears does Kate have ?

6. Jed is 16. He has a younger sister, Anne aged 14.

   Jake's age lies between Jed's and Anne's.

   How old is Jake ?

7.  Last year, Jen bought a 2-year old car.

   How old is the car now ?

8. Nora has £10 in her purse.

   Kate has £1 more than that.

   How much money does Kate have ?

9.  Mary came in 2nd in her school race.

   Lisa came in just after Mary.

   In what position did Lisa come in ?

10. Twenty racing cars started the race.

    a Alec finished in 14th place.

       This was 1 place in front of Ian.

       In what place did Ian finish ?

    b Gary came 2nd last.

       In what position (*1st to 20th*) did Gary finish ?

1. Write down the **larger** number in each :-

   a 16 or 17   b 15 or 12   c 18 or 19.

2. Write down the **smaller** of the two numbers :-

   a 7 or 8   b 13 or 11   c 20 or 18.

3. a   If 1 **more** balloon is added, how
      many balloons will there be then ?

   b If instead there was 1 balloon
      fewer than shown, how many
      would there be ?
      (*Write your answer as a word*).

4. What number is **one more than** :-

   a 6   b 12   c 16   d 19 ?

5. What is the number that is **one less than** :-

   a 4   b 18   c 12   d 17 ?

6. In the theatre, Paul is sitting in the **14th** row.

   Uncle Charlie is sitting in the row in front of him.

   Which row is Uncle Charlie sitting in ?

Number Bonds to 20

Be able to use
addition
up to 20.

Using counters can help you when adding.

Example :-   What is 13 + 6 ?

13

add

6

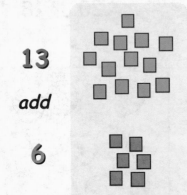

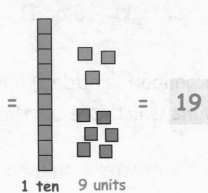

= 19

1 ten   9 units

This can be
written as :-

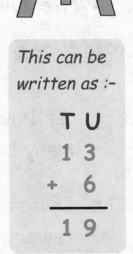

```
  T U
  1 3
+   6
-----
  1 9
```

Exercise 1   *Counters will help in this exercise.*   Worksheet 6·1

1. Copy and complete :-

a   14
    + 2

b   13
    + 4

c   17
    + 2

d   15
    + 4

e   11
    + 3

f   18
    + 2

g   13
    + 5

h   5
   + 10

i   6
   + 11

When adding, you must line up the numbers.

Line up the 2 below the 5

Example :-   Add 15 + 2

2. Add :-

a 14 + 2	b 8 + 10	c 13 + 3
d 12 + 7	e 11 + 4	f 6 + 14
g 10 + 10	h 11 + 4 + 3	i 12 + 3 + 4.

3. Lucy has 12 dolls. Jane has 5 dolls.

   How many dolls altogether ?

4.    Ravi has 11 marbles. Ben has 4.

   How many marbles in total ?

5. A farmer has 15 cows and 5 sheep.

   How many animals does he have ?

6.   Nick has 8 spiders. Ben has 10.

   How many spiders altogether ?

7. There are 12 ducks and
   3 swans in a pond.

   How many birds is that **in total** ?

8.    Tiddles has **4** treats.
   Spot has **14** treats.

   How many treats **altogether** ?

9. A jar has **15** sweets.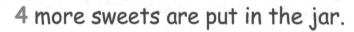

   4 more sweets are put in the jar.

   How many sweets are there in the jar now ?

10. Jemma has **10** red bows.

    Jane has the **same** number of bows.

    How many bows do they have **altogether** ?

11.    Mr Todd has **5** biscuits.
    Mrs Todd has **3** biscuits.
    The children have **9** biscuits.

    How many biscuits do the
    family have ?

Problem Solving (up to 20)

Be able to solve problems with addition to 20.

Counters will help in this exercise.

Examples :- What are the missing numbers ?

14 + ? = 16   7 + ☐ = 18

2 is the missing   11 is the missing
   number.   number.

Exercise 2   *Counters will help in this exercise.*

1. What are the missing numbers ?

   a   12 + ☐ = 15   b   11 + ☐ = 18   c   17 + ☐ = 20

   d   3 + ☐ = 14   e   5 + ☐ = 17   f   3 + ☐ = 19.

2. What are the missing numbers ?

   a   11 + ☐ = 17   b   ☐ + 3 = 18   c   ☐ + 4 = 14

   d   3 + ☐ = 19   e   ☐ + 16 = 17   f   4 + ☐ + 1 = 18.

3. Mr Todd has 7 ties. Mr Duff has some ties.
    Altogether they have 18 ties.

    How many ties does Mr Duff have ?

4.    Ed owns some cars. He buys 13 more.
                          Ed now has 20 cars.

                          How many did Ed start with ?

1. How many in total ?

  a   11
       + 2

  b   12
       + 3

  c   17
       + 2

  d   4
       + 14

  e   10
       + 8

  f   13
       + 7

2. Find :-

  a 16 + 3

  b 11 + 7

  c 14 + 6

  d 5 + 13

  e 3 + 17

  f 11 + 6 + 2.

3. Jack has 6 comics. Jake has 12 comics.

   How many comics altogether ?

4. Find the missing numbers :-

  a 15 + ☐ = 18

  b ☐ + 11 = 17

  c ☐ + 13 + 1 = 20.

5. Mr Duff has some pencils.
   Miss Young has nine pencils.
   Altogether they have twenty pencils.

   How many pencils does Mr Duff have ?

Days of the Week

There are **7** days in each week.

Here is a list of them in order :-

Monday

Tuesday

Wednesday

Thursday

Friday

Saturday

Sunday

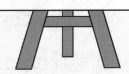

Sun	Mon	Tue	Wed	Thur	Fri	Sat
1	2	3	4	5	6	7
8	9	10	11	12	13	14
15	16	17	18	19	20	21
22	23	24	25	26	27	28
29	30	31				

This is a calendar.

Saturday and **Sunday**
together
make up the **weekend**.

We can use :- Mon - Tue - Wed - Thu - Fri - Sat - Sun.

Exercise 1

1. Copy each neatly **5** times :-

a   Monday (Mo............)   b   Tuesday (Tu............)

c   Wednesday (W...........)   d   Thursday

e   Friday   f   Saturday

g   Sunday.

2. Don't look back. Write all the days of the week :-

Mo....... Tu....... We....... Th........ F........ S........ S.......

3. What are the missing days ?

a   Monday   ....   Wednesday

b   Thursday   ....   Saturday

c   Tuesday   ....   Thursday

d   Friday   ....   Sunday

e   Saturday   ....   Monday.

4. a   What day comes just after Wednesday ?

   b   What day comes just after Saturday ?

   c   What day comes just before Friday ?

5.

   a   What day is today ?

   b   What day was yesterday ?

   c   What day will tomorrow be ?

6. I spent all last weekend at the beach.

   Which 2 days was that ?

7. Which days do you go to school ?

Telling the Time - O'clock

A clock face has the numbers 1 to 12 on it.

The long hand tells the **minutes**.

The small hand points to the **hours**.

When the big hand points up to the 12, it is .... ^{something} o'clock.

Example :-

The big hand points to 12 and the small hand points to 4.

This means it is   4 o'clock.

Exercise 2

1. Write down the time here :-

.... o'clock

2. Write down these times :-

a    b    c

2. d  e  f

3. What are the times on these clocks ?

a  b  c

4. What are the times on these watches ?

a  b  c

5. Ben has to meet Sophie at the clock tower at 4 o'clock.

Is Ben there on time ?

6.

Tonight's show begins at

At what time does the show begin ?

Worksheet 7·1

Telling the Time - Half Past

Recognise and tell the time.
(*Half Past*)

This time, the big hand is pointing to the 6.

The big hand points down to 6.

The small hand is between 2 numbers.

Example :-

The big hand points to 6. The small one is between 3 and 4.

This means it is   half past 3.

Exercise 3

1. Write down the time here :-

half past ......

2. Write down these times :-

a
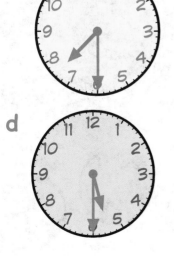

b

c

d

e

f

3. Write down the times on these watches :-

a  b 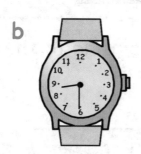 c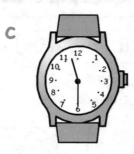

4. Write down these times :-

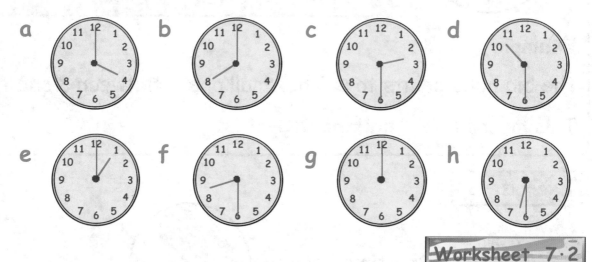

a   b   c   d

e   f   g   h

Worksheet 7·2

5. Write these times in order. Start with the earliest :-

a

3 o'clock   8 o'clock   11 o'clock   7 o'clock   9 o'clock   5 o'clock

b

3 o'clock   4 o'clock   half past 5   6 o'clock   half past 1   half past 2

c

Revisit - Review - Revise

1. Write down the 7 days of the week. Start with **Monday**.

2. a Which day comes just **after** Friday ?

   b Which day comes just **before** Tuesday ?

3. If today is **Sunday**, what day will **tomorrow** be ?

4. Write down these times :-

a

b

c

d

e

f

5. Here are things Ed does one day. Write them **in order**. Start with the **earliest**.

has supper

gets out of bed

goes to school

has breakfast

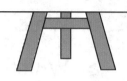

Chapter 8

Recognise and order numbers from 0 to 20.

Revision of Numbers from 0-20

Exercise 1

1. How many insects each time ?

a

b

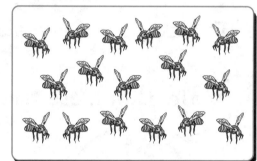

2. What are the missing numbers ?

a 8 ☐ 10 ☐ ☐ ☐ 14 ☐ 16 ☐

b ☐ 18 16 ☐ 12 10 ☐ 6 ☐ 2.

3. What number lies between :-

a 9 and 7   b 15 and 17   c 20 and 18 ?

4. Write down each list, (*highest number first*) :-

a 6 12 9 8   b 18 20 19 16 17.

5. Write down each list, (*lowest number first*) :-

a   11   6   17   13   4   10   15   12

b   15   19   13   11   17   20   14.

6. Write in word form :-

a   7   b   11   c   19

d   13   e   8   f   14.

7. Write each of these as a number :-

a   sixteen   b   nine   c   twelve

d   ten   e   eighteen   f   twenty.

8. Which is the larger number in each :-

a   9 or 8   b   12 or 13   c   17 or 16 ?

9. Write down the smaller of the two numbers :-

a   5 or 7   b   16 or 19   c   13 or 11.

10. Look at the group of numbers below :-

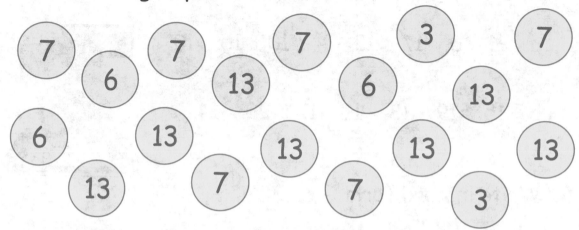

a   Which of these numbers appears **most** ?

b   Which of these numbers appears **least** ?

11. John is seated in the 12th row up from the pitch in the football stand.

His brother is in the row **behind**.

Which row is his brother sitting in ?

12.

Donny has £20 in his wallet.

George has £1 **less** than that.

How much money does George have ?

Recognise and order numbers from 20 to 30.

Each full jar holds 10 sweets.

1 full jar and 7 sweets.   = 17 sweets.

We have 2 full jars   = 20 sweets.

Here, we have
2 full jars and
4 sweets.   = 24 sweets.

	tens	units			
24 means	2	4	=	**2** lots of **ten** and **4** units.

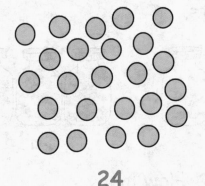

=

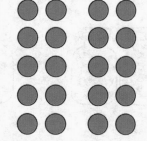

24   10   10   4

1. How many sweets in total each time?

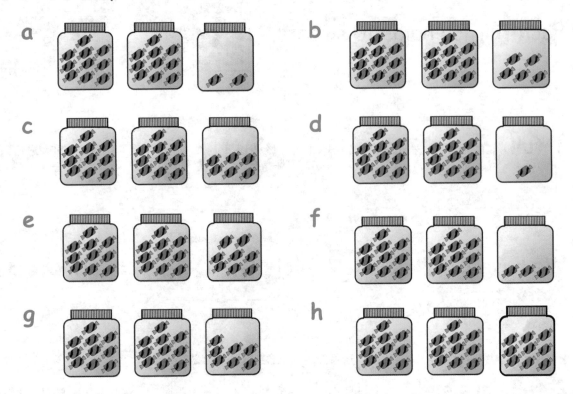

a

b

c

d

e

f

g

h

2. How many sweets in total are in these 3 jars?

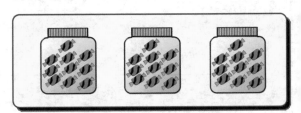

3. Three boys have jars of sweets.

Jay   Toby   Ger

a   Who has the most sweets? How many?

b   Who has the least? How many?

4. Write all the numbers from 30 down to 20.

5. Draw empty jars like this.

Fill them with sweets to show :-

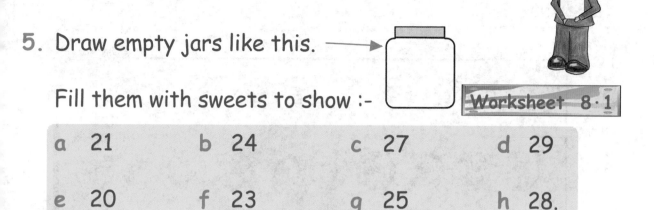

Worksheet 8·1

a 21	b 24	c 27	d 29
e 20	f 23	g 25	h 28.

6. Copy and complete :-

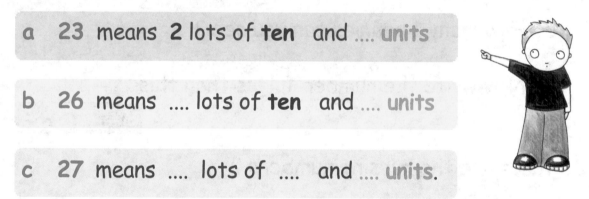

a 23 means **2** lots of **ten** and .... units

b 26 means .... lots of **ten** and .... units

c 27 means .... lots of .... and .... units.

7. Write down all the missing numbers :-

a 21 ☐ 23 24 ☐ 26 27 ☐ 29

b ☐ 29 28 ☐ ☐ 25 24 ☐ 22

c 20 22 24 ☐ 28 ☐

d ☐ 28 26 ☐ ☐ 20.

Exercise 3

1.

a   How many 1 pennies can you see ?

b   Now write the number 1 less than this.

Worksheet 8·2

2. What are the missing numbers ?

a   17   18   ☐   20   ☐   ☐   23   24   ☐

b   ☐   25   ☐   ☐   22   21   20   ☐   18

c   15   ☐   19   ☐   23

d   ☐   25   23   ☐   19

e   24   ☐   ☐   18   ☐ .

19 ☐ 23

3. What number lies between :-

    a   12 and 10   b   23 and 25   c   21 and 19 ?

4. Which two numbers lie between :-

    a   9 and 12   b   21 and 18   c   27 and 30 ?

5. Write each of these numerals in word form :-

a	17	b	16	c	9	d	11
e	18	f	20	g	14	h	13.

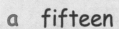

6. Write as a number :-

a	fifteen	b	nineteen	c	four
d	fourteen	e	twelve	f	ten.

7. Copy and complete :-

    a   25 means **2** lots of **ten** and .... units.

    b   12 means .... lot of **ten** and .... units.

7.　c　8　means　.... lots of **ten** and .... units.

d　21　means　.... lots of　.... and .... unit.

e　19　means　.... lot of　.... and .... units.

f　30　means　.... lots of　.... and .... units.

8.　Write each list in order, starting with the **lowest** :-

a　18　23　15　20

b　21　30　19　25　28.

9.　Write each list in order, starting with the **highest** :-

a　17　19　22　14

b　23　18　24　30　26.

10.　What number is **one more than** :-

a　10　　　b　19　　　c　23　　　d　29 ?

11.　What is the number that is **one less than** :-

a　12　　　b　20　　　c　23　　　d　28 ?

12.　Counting up from 20, ... what number is **2 up from 27** ?

13. In a Marathon, Brian finished in **27**th place.

    Tony finished the race just behind Brian.

    What position did Tony finish in ?

14. A box of chocolates has **21** cremes.

    Anna and Lou share them all, but Anna
    gets **1 more** than Lou.

    a   How many sweets did Anna get ?

    b   How many did Lou get ?

15. How many sweets in total are in these 4 jars ?

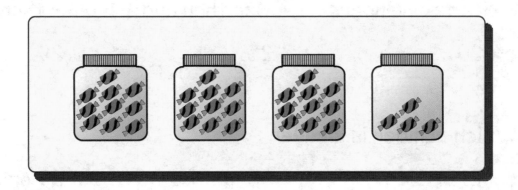

16. In a car race, Brams finished
    in **25th** position.

    Sanna finished 2 places
    in **front** of Brams.

    In what position did Sanna finish ?

1. How many cones ?

2. What numbers are missing ?

a   15   ☐   19   ☐   23   ☐   27

b   ☐   26   ☐   22   ☐   ☐   16.

3. Write two numbers - 1 lower than and 1 higher than :-

a 20   b 25   c 29.

4. Which number is smaller :-

a 21 or 19   b 26 or 14   c 29 or 28 ?

5.

Molly was the 20th customer to enter the shop today.

Daisy followed her in, one behind.

What customer number was Daisy ?

Subtraction within 10 (Pictorially)

Be able to subtract up to 10.

Using counters can help with subtraction.

(Taking away).

Example :-

Ben has 7 Smarties. Lucy *takes away* 3 of them.

How many are left ?

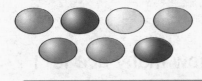 **subtract** (or take away 3)  *gives* 4

| 7 | – | 3 | = | 4. |

Exercise 1

Worksheet 9·1

1. Nick has 3 counters. Ravi *takes* away 2.

   How many are left ?

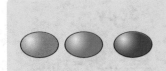 take away 2

Copy

| 3 | – | 2 | = | .... |

2. How many are left ?

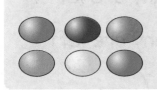 take away 3

Copy

| 6 | – | 3 | = | .... |

3. 5 ducks take away 2 ducks. How many are left ?

take away 2

Copy

5 – ... = ...

4. 8 sweets take away 5 sweets. How many are left ?

take away 5

Copy

8 – ... = ...

5. Ten pencils take away 6 pencils. How many are left ?

take away 6

Copy

10 – ... = ...

6. Eight pins take away 1 pin. How many are left ?

take away 1

Copy

8 – ... = ...

7. a Six pies take away 4 pies. How many are left ?

    b Nine biscuits take away 1. How many are left ?

    c Find 5 – 1.   d Find 8 – 7.

Subtraction within 10

Be able to subtract up to 10.

Counters will help in this exercise.

Examples :-

| 5 – 1 = 4 | 7 – 2 = 5 |

Exercise 2   Counters will help in this exercise.   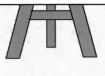 Worksheet 9·2

1. Find 6 take away 2.   **Copy**   6 – 2 = ...

2. Find :-

   a   8 take away 5   b   9 take away 1

   c   5 take away 5   d   6 subtract 1

   e   take 5 from 9   f   take 2 from 10.

3. Subtract :-

   a   8 – 1   b   9 – 0   c   10 – 7

   d   7 – 5   e   6 – 4   f   10 – 8

   g   7 – 3   h   9 – 5   i   10 – 3

   j   9 – 4   k   8 – 8   l   10 – 5.

4. Find :-

   a   8 – 2 – 1   b   6 – 1 – 2   c   7 – 3 – 1

   d   9 – 5 – 1   e   10 – 3 – 5   f   10 – 6 – 4.

5. a   Jack has **7** coins. Lee takes away **2** of them.

How many coins are left ?

b   Sara has **9** coins. She loses **5** of them.

How many coins does she have left ?

6. a

James has **8** toy soldiers.
Sam has **6** toy soldiers.

How many **more** soldiers does
James have than Sam ?

b   Julie has **ten** apples. She gives Jules **5** of them.

How many apples does Julie have now ?

7. Mr Duff has **9** TJ books.
Miss Young has **4** TJ books.

How many **more** books does
Mr Duff have than Miss Young ?

8.

Simon has **9** bananas.
He gives **4** to Pete and **3** to Fern.

How many does Simon have now ?

Problem Solving (up to 10)

Be able to solve problems with subtraction up to 10.

Counters will help in this exercise.

What are the missing numbers ?

$4 - \boxed{?} = 1$

3 is the missing number.

$8 - \boxed{} = 3$

5 is the missing number.

Exercise 3 Counters will help in this exercise.

Worksheet 9·3

1. What are the missing numbers ?

   a $4 - \boxed{} = 3$ b $5 - \boxed{} = 3$ c $7 - \boxed{} = 3$

   d $6 - \boxed{} = 3$ e $9 - \boxed{} = 4$ f $10 - \boxed{} = 4.$

2. What are the missing numbers ?

   a $8 - \boxed{} = 4$ b $\boxed{} - 1 = 6$ c $\boxed{} - 2 = 7$

   d $9 - \boxed{} = 9$ e $\boxed{} - 8 = 0$ f $9 - \boxed{} - 1 = 4.$

3. Ali has **9** goldfish. He gives **3** to Zara.

   How many goldfish does Ali have now ?

4.

   Gio has some cars. Jo takes **2** cars.
   Gio now has **6** cars.

   How many cars did Gio start with ?

1. Ben has **5** Smarties. Jemma takes **3** of them.

   How many Smarties has Ben now ?

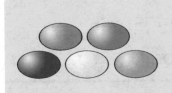 take away 3  Copy

   5 – ... = ...

2. Find :-

   | a | 9 take away 1 | b | 7 take away 5 | c | 5 subtract 2. |

3. Find :-

   a 5 – 4   b 9 – 3   c 10 – 9

   d 6 – 2   e 9 – 6   f 10 – 10

   g 9 – 3 – 2   h 8 – 4 – 3   i 10 – 3 – 7.

4. What are the missing numbers ?

   a 7 – ☐ = 4   b ☐ – 2 = 6   c ☐ – 9 = 1.

5.  Jo has **8** birds.
   She gives some birds to James.
   Jo now has **2** birds.

   How many birds did she give James ?

Chapter 10

Numbers from 30 to 100

Recognise and order numbers from 30 to 100.

The number just after 29 is called 30.

It is written as 30.

(*Three lots of 10*).

	Tens	Units	
30 means	**3**	0	= **3** lots of **ten** and 0 units.

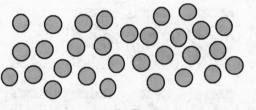

30 = 10 10 10

Each full jar still holds 10 sweets.

3 full jars
and 7 sweets.

T U
= 3 7 sweets.

4 full jars
and 4 sweets.

T U
= 4 4 sweets.

This time we have
5 full jars.

= 50 sweets.

Exercise 1

1. How many sweets ?

   a

   b

   c

   d

   e

2. How many sweets altogether here ?

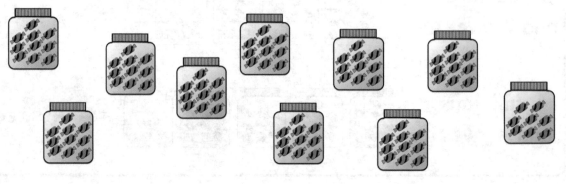

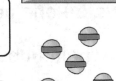

3. Draw empty jars like this. ⟶

Fill them with round sweets to show :-

| a 33 | b 47 | c 56 | d 68. |

4. Copy and complete :-

   a   58   means   **5** lots of **ten**   and .... units.

   b   67   means   .... lots of **ten**   and .... units.

   c   94   means   .... lots of   ....   and .... units.

5. Copy and complete :-

   a   15 =   ☐ 1   ten   and   ☐   units

   b   22 =   ☐   tens and   ☐ 2   units

   c   36 =   ☐   tens and   ☐   units

   d   48 =   ☐   tens and   ☐   units

   e   63 =   ☐   tens and   ☐   units

   f   7 =   ☐   tens and   ☐   units

   g   98 =   ☐   tens and   ☐   units.

6. I have **64** one pence coins.

I put them in bundles of **10** to make **10 pence**.

   a   How many **full** bundles of 10 can I make ?

   b   How many one pence coins will I have left over ?

7. Clive bought **41** daffodil bulbs.

He placed them in pots, with **10** bulbs in each pot.

   a   How many **full** pots of 10 did he get ?

   b   How many bulbs were left to go in the spare pot ?

8. At Oliver's Bus Garage, the coaches must be parked **ten** to a row as they arrive.

There are **75** buses in the garage tonight.

   a How many **full** rows of 10 ?

   b How many buses are parked in a new row ?

Place Value *Extension*

A number can be written in **words** and in **digits**.

("digits" are numbers like 1, 2, 3, 4, ...)

You should be able to change a number from one form to the other.

> Example 1 :-   Eighty six written using digits is 86.
>
> Example 2 :-   73 written in words is seventy three.

Exercise 2

1. Write these numbers using **digits** :-

   a   forty three   b   twenty eight   c   thirty one

   d   sixty five   e   seventy two   f   eighty

   g   eleven   h   ninety   i   sixty nine.

2. Write these numbers using **words** :-

   a   38   b   52   c   86

   d   17   e   70   f   88

   g   97   h   66   i   100.

3. There are 41 giraffes in a zoo.

Write this number in words.

4.  In the same zoo there are eighty seven chimps.

Write this number using digits.

5. Put each list in the correct order.

Start with the lowest.

a 35, 46, 29, 58   b 38, 25, 52, 41, 60

c 72, 63, 59, 84   d 95, 72, 93, 81, 77.

6. Put each list in the correct order.

Start with the highest.

a 23, 37, 35, 44   b 47, 51, 62, 59, 50

c 69, 78, 85, 81   d 93, 89, 91, 88, 90.

7. What number is 1 before and what number is 1 after :-

a 79   b 90   c 32   d 99 ?

Missing Numbers

Example 1 :-

What are the missing numbers in the list below ?

65   67   69 ↑ 71   75   79   .....

going up **2** at a time

You should see a pattern of numbers going up in 2's.

The missing numbers are :- 73, 77 and 81.

Example 2 :-

What number is **1** down and what number is **1** up from :-

Exercise 3

1.   Write down all the missing numbers :-

a   21   23   24   26   27   29

b   12   13   16   18   19   22

c   24   23   21   19   18   ....   15.

2. Copy this grid of numbers.

   Fill in all the missing numbers :-

0	1	2	3	.....	5	.....	7	8	.....
10	11	12	.....	14	.....	16	17	.....	19
20	21	.....	23	.....	25	26	.....	28	.....
30	.....	32	33	.....	.....	36	.....	38	39
.....	.....	42	43	.....	45	.....	.....	48	.....
50	.....	52	.....	.....	.....	56	.....	.....	59
.....	61	.....	63	.....	65	.....	67	.....	.....
70	.....	.....	.....	.....	75	.....	77	.....	79
80	.....	.....	83	.....	.....	86	.....	88	.....
.....	92	.....	.....	95	.....	.....	.....	.....	.....

3. What is the number which comes just after 99 ?

4. Write down all the missing numbers :-

   a   51   52   54   56   59   ....

   b   70   71   74   77   ....

   c   84   85   86   88   91   ....

4. d 57 58 .... 61 .... 63 .... 65 ....

e 83 .... 81 79   f 42 .... 40 38

g 68 .... 66 ....   h .... 97 .... 99 ....

5. Write down all the numbers that are missing.

a 56 58 62   b 44 46 52

c 84 82 78   d 60 .... 56 54 ....

e 92 .... 88 84   f .... 97 95 ....

6. Some numbers have fallen off these beach huts.

36 38 42

Write down the missing hut numbers.

7. This special dartboard should have all the numbers from **61** to **72** on it.

Write down all the numbers that are missing from the board.

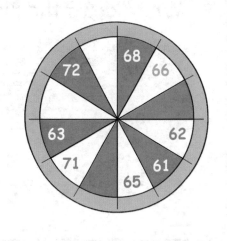

Revisit - Review - Revise

1. How many sweets in total are in the jars ?

2. Angela has **76** strawberries.

   She puts them in glasses, **10** in each,
   along with ice cream.

   a   How many **full** glasses of 10 will she get ?

   b   How many extra strawberries will she have ?

3. a   For the number **82**, how many **tens** does it have ?

   b   For the number **67**, how many **units** has it ?

4. Write down the missing numbers :-

a	57	58	.....	.....	61	62	.....	64	.....

b	96	.....	92	.....	88	86	84	.....	80

c	13	15	.....	19	.....	23	25	.....	..... .

Chapter 11

Subtraction 2

Subtraction up to 20

Be able to use subtraction up to 20.

Using counters can help you when subtracting.

Example :-   What is 13 – 6 ?

13

take away

6

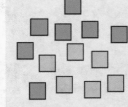

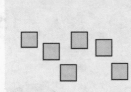

 = **7**

This can be written as :-

```
 T U
 1 3
-   6
―――
   7
```

Exercise 1

Worksheet 11·1

1. Copy and complete :-

a	11 – 2		b	13 – 4		c	17 – 2
d	14 – 4		e	11 – 3		f	18 – 2
g	13 – 5		h	15 – 9		i	16 – 6

When **subtracting**, you must **line up** the numbers.

Line up the 2 below the 5

```
T U
1 5
-   2
─────
1 3
```

Example :-   **Find** 15 – 2.

2. Find :-

a   16 – 2   b   17 – 7   c   15 – 4

d   12 – 7   e   11 – 4   f   16 – 14

g   16 – 7   h   16 – 4 – 3   i   18 – 6 – 4.

3. Ed has **16** lollies. Jo takes **5** of them.

How many lollies does Ed have now ?

4.

Jane has **14** bags.
She gives **6** bags to Jemma.

How many bags does Jane have now ?

5. Spot has **15** collars.

Eight are worn and thrown away.

How many collars does Spot have now ?

6. a Jane has **17** coins. Lucy takes away **5** coins.

   How many coins does Jane have now ?

   b The girls have **15** coins.
   They give **8** coins to the boys.

   How many coins do the girls have now ?

7. a

   Jim has **13** cans of juice.
   Sam has **4** cans of juice.

   How many **more** does Jim have ?

   b Jo has **19** toy animals.
   She gives **8** to her little brother.

   How many animals does Jo have now ?

8. Mr Duff has **twenty** marker pens.
   Miss Young has **nine**.

   What is the **difference** in the
   number of pens ? (*Hint - subtract*).

9.

   Two boys have **9** cakes **each**.
   They each give away **5** cakes.

   How many cakes **in total** do the
   boys have now ?

Problem Solving (up to 20)

Be able to solve problems with subtraction to 20.

Counters will help in this exercise.

What are the missing numbers ?

$14 - \boxed{?} = 11$ $17 - \boxed{} = 4$

$\boxed{3}$ is the missing number. $\boxed{13}$ is the missing number.

Exercise 2   *Counters will help in this exercise.*   **Worksheet 11·2**

1. What are the missing numbers ?

   a $12 - \boxed{} = 10$ b $11 - \boxed{} = 8$ c $17 - \boxed{} = 7$

   d $13 - \boxed{} = 4$ e $15 - \boxed{} = 7$ f $19 - \boxed{} = 8.$

2. What are the missing numbers ?

   a $12 - \boxed{} = 5$ b $\boxed{} - 3 = 11$ c $\boxed{} - 4 = 10$

   d $13 - \boxed{} = 2$ e $\boxed{} - 6 = 11$ f $14 - \boxed{} - 1 = 8.$

3. Mr Todd has 17 dice. He gives Mr Duff 9 dice.

   How many dice does Mr Todd have now ?

4.

            Tom has some DVDs.
            He gives Ed **nine** of them.
            Tom now has 8 DVDs left.

            How many did Tom start with ?

1. Copy and complete :-

a   16
    - 4
                b   14
                    - 5
                            c   17
                                - 9

d   13
    - 6
                e   14
                    - 7
                            f   12
                                - 8

2. Find :-

a   15 – 4   b   12 – 4   c   11 – 7

d   12 – 6   e   18 – 9   f   16 – 8.

3. Jane has **17** posters. She gives **8** of them to Nick.

   How many posters does Jane have now ?

4. What are the missing numbers ?

   a   12 – ☐ = 9   b   11 – ☐ = 3   c   ☐ – 6 = 7.

5. Bob has some pencils. Bev takes **six** of them.
   Bob now has **fourteen** pencils left.

   How many pencils did Bob start with ?

Our Coins

Recognise the coins we use every day.

Here are the coins which we use every day :-

1p piece   2p piece   5p piece   10p piece

20p piece   50p piece   £1 coin   £2 coin

Example 1 :-

    is the same as   

Example 2 :-

    is the same as

Example 3 :-

   is the same as   

1. How many are in   ?

2. How many are in  ?

3. How many are in  ?

4. How many are in  ?

5. How many  are in  ?

6. How many  are in  ?

7. How many  are in ?

8. How many 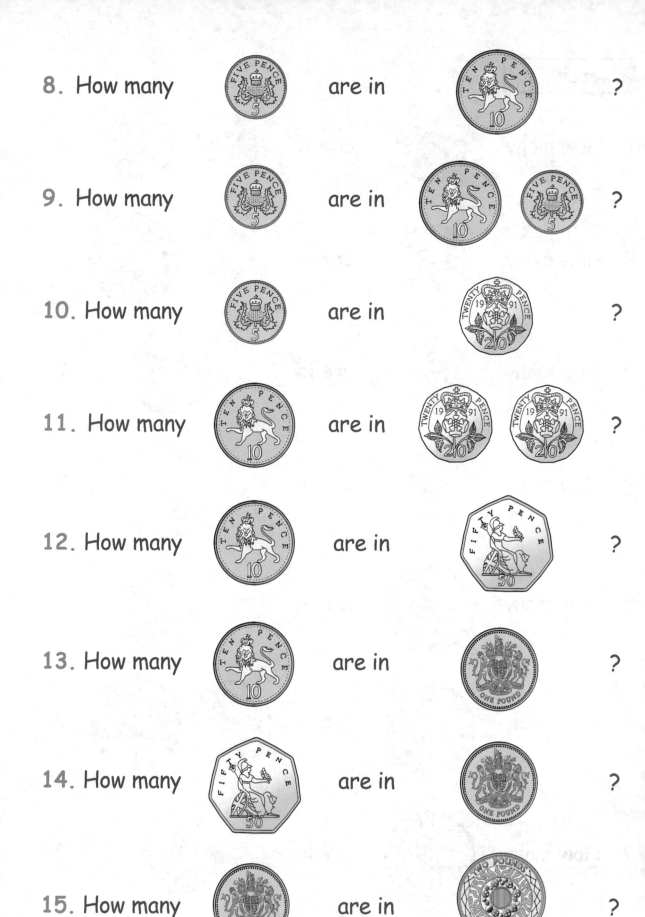 are in ？

9. How many are in ？

10. How many are in ？

11. How many are in ？

12. How many are in ？

13. How many are in ？

14. How many are in ？

15. How many are in ？

What does each cost ?

1.
pencil

2.
pencil
sharpener

3.
some
screws

4.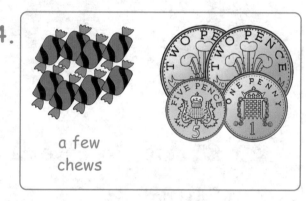
a few
chews

5.
fudge cake

6.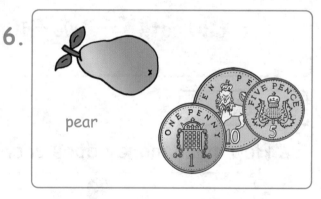
pear

7.
dark
chocolate

8.
crisps

Our Notes

Here are some of the notes we use every day :-

a £5 note   =   Five £1 coins

a £10 note =   Two £5 notes   = Ten £1 coins

a £20 note =   Two £10 notes = Twenty £1 coins

Exercise 3

1. How much money does each boy have ?

a

Dave

b

Jed

1.

c

Colin

d

Eddie

e

Frank

f

Gerry

g

Abdul

h

Tony

2. What colour are these coins :- (**bronze**, *silver* or *gold* ?)

   a 5 pence   b 2 pence   c £1 ?

3. Which coins are **not** round ?

4. What is the main colour on a £10 note ?

Mr Piggy Bank

5. Which coin has got gold and silver colouring ?

6. Why might you prefer a £10 note than ten £1 coins ?

7. James has **ten** 50p coins.

   What note could he change them for ?

8. What is the value of each of these coins ?

a   b    c    d

e    f   g    h

9. Find out how long a £5 note lasts before it is returned to the bank and a new one printed.

1. How many are in ?

2. How many  are in  ?

3. How many are in   ?

4. What is the price of this ice cream cone ?

5. I bought this soft toy with the money shown.

   What did it cost ?

6. What animal is on one face of a 10p coin ?

7. How many edges has a 50p coin ?

More Missing Numbers

If the numbers are all mixed up, put them in order first.

Example :- What is the missing counter number here ?

(31)   (36)   (38)   (32)
   (34)   (40)
(35)   (33)   (30)   (39)

Order them :-

(30) (31) (32) (33) (34) (35) (36)   (38) (39) (40)

The missing counter has to be **37** :-   (37).

Exercise 1

1.   What are the missing house numbers ?

2.   What numbers are 1 down and 1 up from :-

a | .... 65 .... | b | .... 38 .... | c | .... 50 .... | d | .... 99 .... | ?

3. These cars are numbered 70 to 79.

   What are the missing numbers ? (*hint - put them in order*).

4. These boats are numbered 91 to 100.

   What are the 4 missing numbers ?

5. These 10 friends enter a charity race.

   They are given race numbers 30 to 39.

   What are the missing race numbers ?

6. These cards are numbered **in order**.

   The **smallest** card is card number 75.

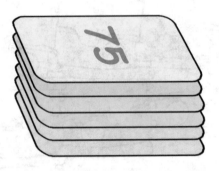 

   What will the number be on the **bottom** card ?

7. What are the numbers **2 down** and **2 up** from :-

   a   ┌──────────────┐
        │ .... 47 .... │
        └──────────────┘

   b   ┌──────────────┐
        │ .... 78 .... │
        └──────────────┘

   c   ┌──────────────┐
        │ .... 60 .... │
        └──────────────┘

   d   ┌──────────────┐
        │ .... 81 .... │ ?
        └──────────────┘

8. Ger lives on the **23rd** floor of this skyscraper building.

   a   His friend, Ian, lives **2 floors down** from him.

        On what floor does Ian live ?

   b   Ger's other friend, Eva, lives **two floors above** him.

        On what floor does Eva live ?

Recognise where numbers should be placed on a scale.

Worksheet 13·2

1. What number is the arrow pointing to ?

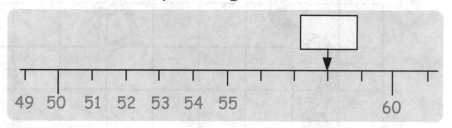

49 50 51 52 53 54 55   60

2. What numbers are the arrows pointing to ? (A is .....)

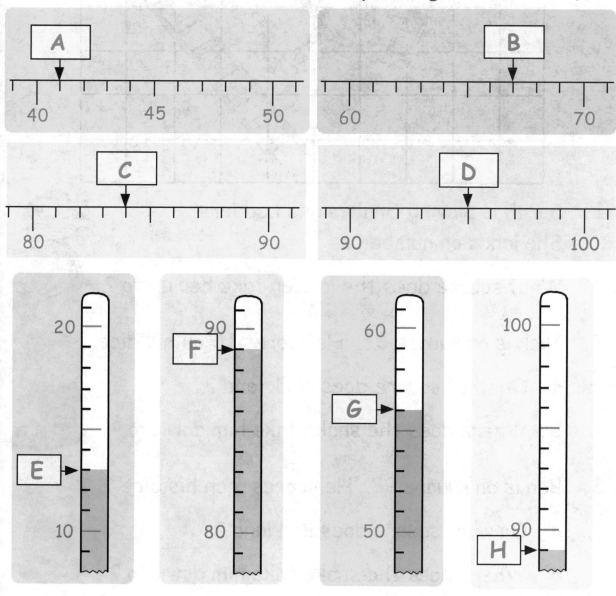

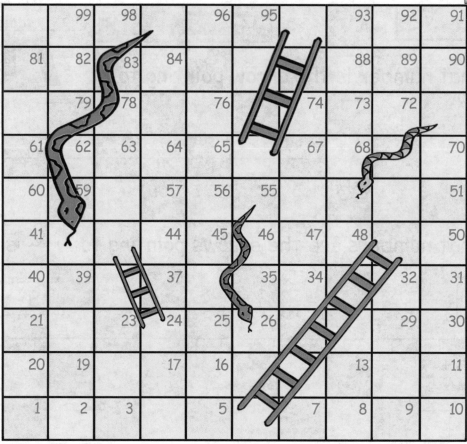

1. Sarah is playing Snakes and Ladders.
    She lands on number 6.

    What square does the ladder take her up to ?

2. Nick is on square 61. He scores 10 on his dice.

    a   On what square does Nick land ?

    b   Where does the snake take him down to ?

3. Ben is on square 92. He scores 5 on his dice.

    a   On what square does Ben land ?

    b   Where does the snake take him down to ?

More Than / Less Than

Find the number 1 more than or 1 less than a given number.

Example 1 :-

What is the number **one more** than 47 ?

> Think of the numbers in the 40's :-
>
>
>
> 40 41 42 ....
>
> You will soon reach 47, with **one more** giving **48**.

Example 2 :-

What is the number **one less** than 95 ?

> Think of the numbers in the 90's :-
>
> 90 91 92 ....
>
> You will soon reach 95.
>
> The number will be just **before** 95, which is **94**.

*You may be asked to find :-

just after, 1 up from **or** one above,   *same as one more.*

just before, 1 down from **or** one fewer,   *same as one less.*

1. What number comes just after :-

   a   45   b 73   c   67   d   89 ?

2. What number comes just before :-

   a   32   b 50   c   78   d   99 ?

3. Write the number which is one more than :-

   a   57   b 61   c   74   d   39.

4. Write the number which is one less than :-

   a   20   b 71   c   95   d   100.

5. Craig caught 60 fish.

   Simon caught 1 fish fewer.

   How many fish did Simon catch ?

6. In a maths test, Pria got 68 marks out of 70.

   Debbie beat Pria by 1 mark.

   What did Debbie score out of 70 ?

Revisit - Review - Revise

1. The bins in Glebe Street are numbered 86 to 94.

What are the missing numbers ?

2. What numbers are arrows **A** and B pointing to ?

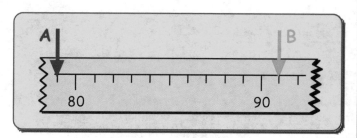

3. What are the numbers 2 down and 2 up from :-

.... 61 ....

4. What is one more than 97 ?

5. A thermometer measures temperature in degrees.

What temperature is one degree below 80 degrees ?

6. George has a collection of 40 T-shirts.

Martin has one T-shirt fewer.

How many does Martin have ?

0 - Revision - *Page 1*

a

a

b

b

Sarah.

pen

basin.

a 5   b 10

a 3   b 5

a 8.   b 7

2 3 5 6 8 10

a 5   b 7

7

5.

a [ ]   b ↓

a square   b rectangle
c circle   d triangle
a cube   b cone
c pyramid   d cylinder
a apple   b banana
c melon
a cone   b cylinder
c cuboid
a goat b horse c sheep d cow
a 9   b 4   c 3
a 4   b 5   c 18   d 3

1 - Whole No's 1 - *Page 6*

1 - Exercise 1 - *Page 6*

a 6   b 8   c 7   d 9
e 8   f 10   g 5   h 9
i 6   j 8   k 7   l 9
m 9   n 10
a 3   b 9   c 8   d 6
e 1   f 7   g 5   h 10
i 4   j 2   k 1   l 0
a 4 6 8 9
b 2 4 5 10
c 2 3 7 9
d 1 3 5 7 9
e 8 6 4 2
f 9 7 6 5 2
g 2   h 4   i 8
j 9   k 1 3 l 9 8

4. a 4   b 1   c 8
    d 9   e 3   f 5
5. a 5 6 b 2 3 c 5 4
    d 8 7 e 8 9 f 7 6
6. a 2 4 6 7
    b 1 5 8 9 10
    c 3 4 7 8 9
    d 4 6 7 8 9 10
7. a 6 5 3 2
    b 9 8 7 4 2
    c 10 9 8 7
    d 9 8 7 5 4 2
8. a 2 4 8
    b 9 7 1

Ch 1 - Exercise 2 - *Page 11*

1. a six b eight c four d seven
    e three f nine g two   h ten.
2. a 7   b 1   c 9   d 6
    e 10   f 5   g 3   h 8
3. ten nine eight seven six five
    four three two one zero

Ch 2 - Addition 1 - *Page 13*

Ch 2 - Exercise 1 - *Page 13*

1. 3 + 2 = 5   2. 6 + 3 = 9
3. 5 + 2 = 7   4. 3 + 3 = 6
5. 4 + 3 = 7   6. 2 + 7 = 9
7. 5 + 5 = 10

Ch 2 - Exercise 2 - *Page 15*

1. 4 + 2 = 6
2. a 2 + 6 = 8
    b 8 + 1 = 9
    c 4 + 3 = 7
3. a 7 + 1 = 8
    b 9 + 0 = 9
    c 1 + 5 = 6
4. a 5   b 8   c 9
    d 7   e 9   f 10
5. a 6   b 6   c 7
    d 8   e 8   f 10
6. a 9   b 8
7. a 7   b 9
8. 10
9. a 6   b 10

Ch 2 - Exercise 3 - *Page 17*

1. a 3   b 7   c 3
    d 6   e 2   f 7
2. a 1   b 5   c 6
    d 2   e 1   f 3
3. 5
4. 8

Ch 3 - Whole No's 2 - *Page 19*

Ch 3 - Exercise 1 - *Page 19*

1. a 13   b 16   c 12
2. a 12   b 17   c 13
    d 14   e 20   f 16
    g 19   h 15   i 17
3. a 11   b 13   c 15
    d 10   e 12   f 14
4. Jars with sweets in them :-
    a 11   b 15   c 13   d 17
    e 19   f 12   g 20   h 18
5. a 13 16 18 20
    b 12 13 14 16 19 20
    c 11 13 14 16 18 20
    d 18 16 14 13
    e 19 17 16 15 13
    f 20 18 16 15 12 11
    g 12 14   h 14 16 17
    i 19 18 16
    j 20 18 17 16 14
6. a 11   b 16   c 15
    d 19   e 18   f 12
7. a 12 13   b 17 18
    c 16 15   d 19 18
    e 11 10   f 16 17
8. a 12 14 15 17
    b 10 11 13 18 20
    c 14 16 17 18
    d 11 13 14 16 17
9. a 16 15 13 12
    b 19 18 17 16 14
    c 20 18 14 11
    d 18 16 15 14 13
10. a 10 12 16
    b 19 17 11 7

Ch 3 - Exercise 2 - *Page 24*

1. a sixteen   b eighteen
   c fourteen   d seventeen
   e thirteen   f nineteen
   g twelve   h twenty
2. a 17   b 11   c 19   d 16
   e 12   f 15   g 13   h 18
3. twenty   nineteen   eighteen
   seventeen   sixteen   fifteen
   fourteen   thirteen   twelve
   eleven   ten   nine   eight
   seven   six   five   four
   three   two   one   zero

Ch 4 - 2-D Shapes - *Page 26*

Ch 4 - Exercise 1 - *Page 26*

1. square
2. rectangle
3. triangle
4. circle
5. a 6   b 4   c 3   d 4
   e 2   f 2   g 0
6. a circle
   b triangle & circles
   c rectangle
   d triangles & rectangles
   e triangle & rectangle
   f circles   g rectangles
   h squares
7. 2 squares,   4 rectangles,
   1 circle,   1 triangle
8. See drawings
9. Various
10. Various

Ch 4 - Exercise 2 - *Page 29*

1.

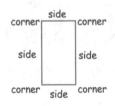

2.

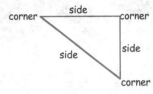

3.

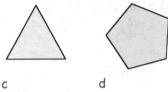

4. a 1   b 0.
5. a 4   b 4   c 3.
6. a 4   b 4   c 3
7. a 5   b 5   c pentagon
8. a 6   b 6   c hexagon
9. a 7   b 7
10. a B, C, E   b F
    c D   d G
11. a   b

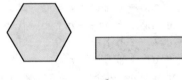

c   d

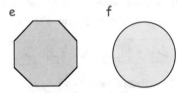

e   f

Ch 5 - Whole No's 3 - *Page 33*

Ch 5 - Exercise 1 - *Page 33*

1. a 9   b 10   c 16
   d 20   e 13   f 14
2. a 5   b 11   c 15
   d 14   e 14   f 12
3. a box with 10 beach balls
   b box with 14 suns
   c box with 12 apples
   d box with 17 ducks
4. a 10   b 14   c 12   d 17
5. a 8   b 13   c 11   d 17
6. a 8   b 12   c 19   d 16
   e 13   f 20   g 14   h 11
7. a 16   b 2   c 17   d 8
   e 11   f 15   g 11   h 12
8. a red   b green   c same
9. a hotdog b Ben   c Lucy

Ch 5 - Exercise 2 - *Page 37*

1. 14
2. 19
3. 13
4. 17°
5. 14
6. 15
7. 3
8. £11
9. 3rd
10. a 15th   b 19th

Ch 6 - Addition 2 - *Page 40*

Ch 6 - Exercise 1 - *Page 40*

1. a 16   b 17   c 19
   d 19   e 14   f 20
   g 18   h 15   i 17
2. a 16   b 18   c 16
   d 19   e 15   f 20
   g 20   h 18   i 19
3. 17
4. 15
5. 20
6. 18
7. 15
8. 18
9. 19
10. 20
11. 17

Ch 6 - Exercise 2 - *Page 43*

1. a 3   b 7   c 3
   d 11   e 12   f 16
2. a 6   b 15   c 10
   d 16   e 1   f 13
3. 11
4. 7 cars

Ch 7 - Time - *Page 45*

Ch 7 - Exercise 1 - *Page 45*

1. a Monday (5 times)
   b Tuesday (5 times)
   c Wednesday (5 times)
   d Thursday (5 times)
   e Friday (5 times)
   f Saturday (5 times)
   g Sunday (5 times)
2. Monday, Tuesday, Wednesday
   Thursday, Friday, Saturday,
   Sunday

Column 1

a Tuesday   b Friday
c Wednesday   d Saturday
e Sunday
a Thursday   b Sunday
c Thursday
a/b/c   Various
Saturday & Sunday
Monday, Tuesday, Wednesday,
Thursday, Friday

7 - Exercise 2 - *Page 47*

2 o'clock
a 5 o'clock   b 8 o'clock
c 1 o'clock   d 3 o'clock
e 7 o'clock   f 9 o'clock.
a 6 o'clock   b 10 o'clock
c 11 o'clock
a 5 o'clock   b 8 o'clock
c 10 o'clock
Yes
7 o'clock

7 - Exercise 3 - *Page 49*

half past 1
a half past 7   b half past 10
c half past 2   d half past 5
e half past 12   f half past 9
a half past 4   b half past 8
c half past 11
a 4 o'clock   b 8 o'clock
c half past 2   d half past 10
e 1 o'clock   f half past 8
g 12 o'clock   h half past 6
a 3 o'clock   5 o'clock   7 o'clock
    8 o'clock   9 o'clock   11 o'clock
b half past 1   half past 2
    3 o'clock   4 o'clock
    half past 5   6 o'clock.
c 2 o'clock   3 o'clock
    half past 3   5 o'clock
    half past 6   8 o'clock

8 - Whole No's 4 - *Page 52*

8 - Exercise 1 - *Page 52*

a 11   b 17
a 9, 11, 12, 13, 15, 17
b 20, 14, 8, 4
a 8   b 16   c 19
a 12, 9, 8, 6
b 20, 19, 18, 17, 16

Column 2

5. a 4, 6, 10, 11, 12, 13, 15, 17
    b 11, 13, 14, 15, 17, 19, 20
6. a seven   b eleven
    c nineteen   d thirteen
    e eight   f fourteen
7. a 16   b 9   c 12
    d 10   e 18   f 20
8. a 9   b 13   c 17
9. a 5   b 16   c 11
10. a 13   b 3
11. 13th
12. £19

Ch 8 - Exercise 2 - *Page 56*

1. a 22   b 25   c 26   d 21
    e 28   f 23   g 27   h 29
2. 30
3. a Jay 28   b Toby 24
4. 30, 29, 28, 27, 26, 25, 24, 23,
    22, 21, 20
5. See diagrams
6. a 23 is 2 lots of ten and 3 units
    b 26 is 2 lots of ten and 6 units
    c 27 is 2 lots of ten and 7 units
7. a 22, 25, 28
    b 30, 27, 26, 23
    c 26, 30
    d 30, 24, 22

Ch 8 - Exercise 3 - *Page 58*

1. a 27   b 26
2. a 19, 21, 22, 25
    b 26, 24, 23, 19
    c 17, 21
    d 27, 21
2. e 22, 20, 16
3. a 11   b 24   c 20
4. a 10 11 b 20 19 c 28 29
5. a seventeen   b sixteen
    c nine   d eleven
    e eighteen   f twenty
    g fourteen   h thirteen
6. a 15   b 19   c 4
    d 14   e 12   f 10
7. a 25 is 2 lots of ten and 5 units
    b 12 is 1 lot of ten and 2 units
    c 8 is 0 lots of ten and 8 units
    d 21 is 2 lots of ten and 1 units
    e 19 is 1 lot of ten and 9 units
    f 30 is 3 lots of ten and 0 units
8. a 15, 18, 20, 23
    b 19, 21, 25, 28, 30

Column 3

9. a 22, 19, 17, 14
    b 30, 26, 24, 23, 18
10. a 11   b 20   c 24   d 30
11. a 11   b 19   c 22   d 27
12. 29
13. 28th
14. a 11   b 10
15. 34
16. 23rd

Ch 9 - Subtraction 1 - *Page 63*

Ch 9 - Exercise 1 - *Page 63*

1. 1
2. 3
3. 3
4. 3
5. 4
6. 7
7. a 2   b 8   c 4   d 1

Ch 9 - Exercise 2 - *Page 65*

1. 4
2. a 3   b 8   c 0
    d 5   e 4   f 8
3. a 7   b 9   c 3
    d 2   e 2   f 2
    g 4   h 4   i 7
    j 5   k 0   l 5
4. a 5   b 3   c 3
    d 3   e 2   f 0
5. a 5   b 4
6. a 2   b 5
7. 5
8. 2

Ch 9 - Exercise 3 - *Page 67*

1. a 1   b 3   c 4
    d 3   e 5   f 6
2. a 4   b 7   c 9
    d 0   e 8   f 4
3. 6
4. 8

Ch 10 - Whole No's 5 - *Page 70*

Ch 10 - Exercise 1 - *Page 70*

1. a 48   b 45   c 70
    d 73   e 86
2. 98
3. See diagrams

4. a 58 is 5 lots of ten and 8 units
   b 67 is 6 lots of ten and 7 units
   c 94 is 9 lots of ten and 4 units
5. a 1 ten and 5 units
   b 2 tens and 2 units
   c 3 tens and 6 units
   d 4 tens and 8 units
   e 6 tens and 3 units
   f 0 tens and 7 units
   g 9 tens and 8 units
6. a 6   b 4
7. a 4   b 1
8. a 7   b 5

Ch 10 - Exercise 2 - Page 73

1. a 43   b 28   c 31
   d 65   e 72   f 80
   g 11   h 90   i 69
2. a thirty eight   b fifty two
   c eighty six   d seventeen
   e seventy   f eighty eight
   g ninety seven   h sixty six
   i one hundred
3. forty one
4. 87
5. a 29, 35, 46, 58
   b 25, 38, 41, 52, 60
   c 59, 63, 72, 84
   d 72, 77, 81, 93, 95
6. a 44, 37, 35, 23
   b 62, 59, 51, 50, 47
   c 85, 81, 78, 69
   d 93, 91, 90, 89, 88
7. a 78, 80   b 89, 91
   c 31, 33   d 98, 100

Ch 10 - Exercise 3 - Page 75

1. a 22, 25, 28
   b 14, 15, 17, 20, 21
   c 22, 20, 17, 16
2. See grid
3. 100
4. a 53, 55, 57, 58, 60
   b 72, 73, 75, 76, 78, 79
   c 87, 89, 90, 92, 93
   d 59, 60, 62, 64, 66
   e 82, 80   f 41, 39
   g 67, 65, 64   h 96, 98, 100
5. a 60   b 48, 50
   c 80   d 58, 52
   e 90, 86   f 99, 93, 91

6. 40, 44, 46
7. 64, 67, 69, 70

Ch 11 - Subtraction 2 - Page 79

Ch 11 - Exercise 1 - Page 79

1. a 9   b 9   c 15
   d 10   e 8   f 16
   g 8   h 6   i 10
2. a 14   b 10   c 11
   d 5   e 7   f 2
   g 9   h 9   i 8
3. 11
4. 8
5. 7
6. a 12   b 7
7. a 9   b 11
8. 11
9. 8

Ch 11 - Exercise 2 - Page 82

1. a 2   b 3   c 10
   d 9   e 8   f 11
2. a 7   b 14   c 14
   d 11   e 17   f 5
3. 8
4. 17

Ch 12 - Money - Page 84

Ch 12 - Exercise 1 - Page 85

1. 6
2. 7
3. 10
4. 50
5. 5
6. 6
7. 10
8. 2
9. 3
10. 4
11. 4
12. 5
13. 10
14. 2
15. 2

Ch 12 - Exercise 2 - Page 87

1. 7p
2. 13p
3. 7p

4. 10p
5. 13p
6. 16p
7. 15p
8. 17p

Ch 12 - Exercise 3 - Page 88

1. a £7   b £8   c £10   d £
   e £13   f £18   g £17   h £
2. a silver b bronze c gold
3. 20p, 50p
4. brown
5. £2 coin
6. easier to carry
7. £5 note
8. a 5p   b 2p   c 20p   d £
   e 50p   f 1p   g 10p   h £
9. between one and five years

Ch 13 - Whole No's 6 - Page

Ch 13 - Exercise 1 - Page 92

1. 39, 40, 42
2. a 64, 66   b 37, 39
   c 49, 51   d 98, 100
3. 74, 78
4. 93, 95, 98, 100
5. 33, 36, 39
6. 80
7. a 45, 49   b 76, 80
   c 58, 62   d 79, 83
8. a 21st b 25th

Ch 13 - Exercise 2 - Page 95

1. 58
2. A 41   B 67   C 84   D 9
   E 13   F 89   G 56   H 8

Ch 13 - Exercise 3 - Page 96

1. 49
2. a 71   b 53
3. a 97   b 42

Ch 13 - Exercise 4 - Page 98

1. a 46   b 74   c 68   d 9
2. a 31   b 49   c 77   d 9
3. a 58   b 62   c 75   d 4
4. a 19   b 70   c 94   d 9
5. 59
6. 69